AF587965

PEGASUS ENCYCLOPEDIA LIBRARY

Chemistry

ELEMENTS AND COMPOUNDS

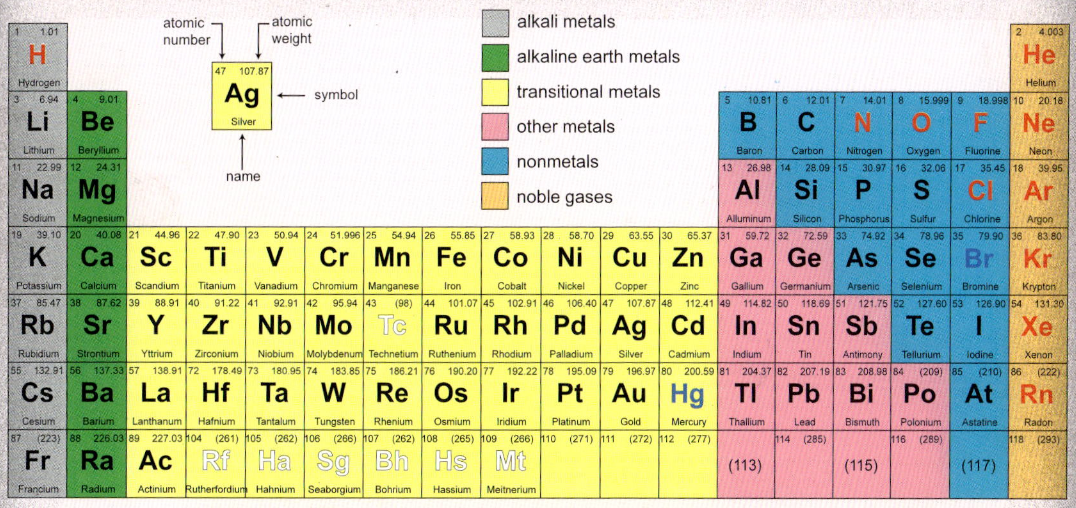

Edited by: Anil Kumar Tomar & Pallabi B. Tomar

Managing editor: Tapasi De

Designed by: Vijesh Chahal, Anil Kumar and Rohit Kumar

Illustrated by: Suman S. Roy, Tanoy Choudhury

Colouring done by: Vinay Kumar, Sonu, Kiran Kumari & Pradeep Kumar

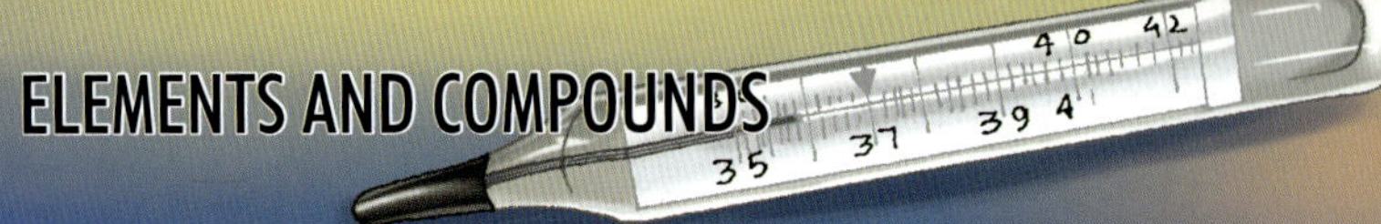

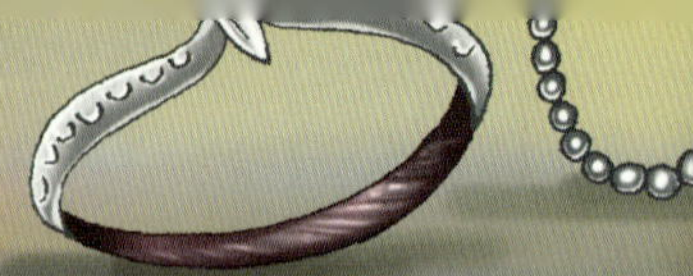

CONTENTS

Introduction..3

Periodic table..5

Element groups 10

Some important elements................................... 17

Test Your Memory..31

Index...32

Introduction

Most forms of matter that we encounter, for example, solid, liquid or gas, are not chemically pure. We can, however, separate these kinds of matter into different pure substances. A pure substance is matter that has distinct properties and a composition that doesn't vary from sample to sample. Water and ordinary table salt are examples of pure substances. All pure substances are either elements or compounds. Elements cannot be decomposed into simpler substances and each element is composed of only one kind of atom. On the other hand, compounds are substances composed of two or more elements in fixed ratio. For example, hydrogen and oxygen are elements while water is a compound composed of hydrogen and oxygen. If the compounds have no fixed ratio of elements, they are referred as **mixtures**.

Elements

It is defined as a substance that cannot be further reduced to simpler substances by ordinary processes. Elements are made up of particles of only one kind. An atom is the smallest particle of an element, which has all the properties of the element. Elements are broadly divided into metals, nonmetals, noble gases and metalloids based on their properties. There are 114 elements known. Out of these 92 of them occur in nature. For example, hydrogen and oxygen.

Compounds

Most elements interact with other elements to form compounds. The constituent elements in a compound are in a fixed proportion by weight. For example, hydrogen gas burns in oxygen gas to form water. Pure water, regardless of its

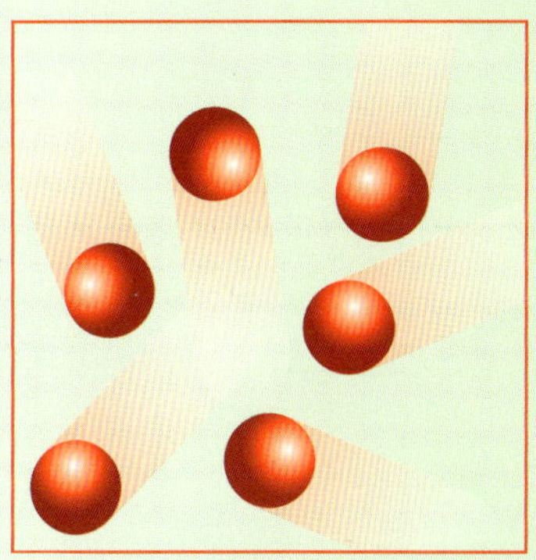
(a) Atoms of an element

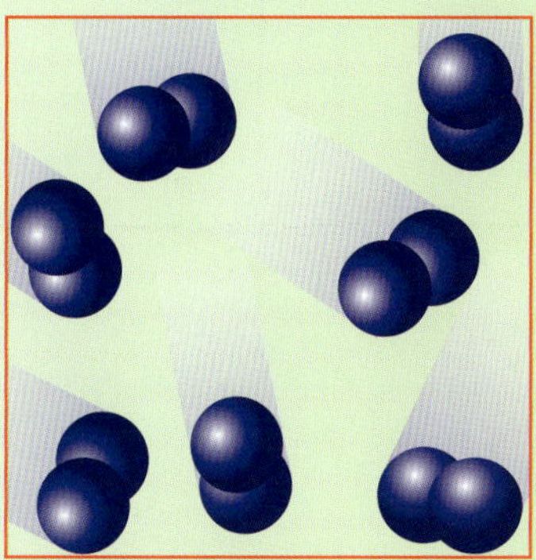
(b) Molecules of an element

(b) Molecules of a compound

(b) Molecules of elements and a compound

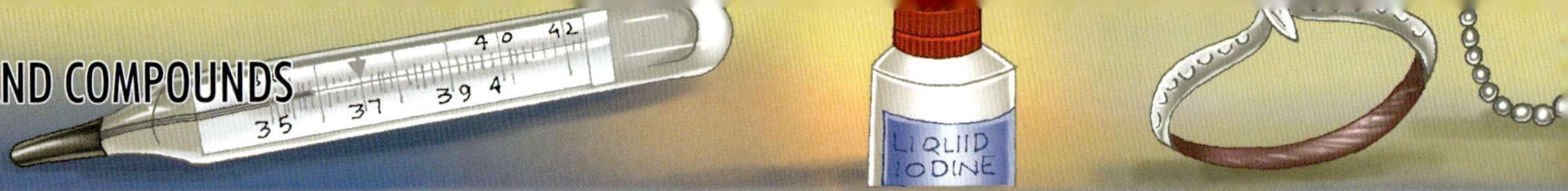

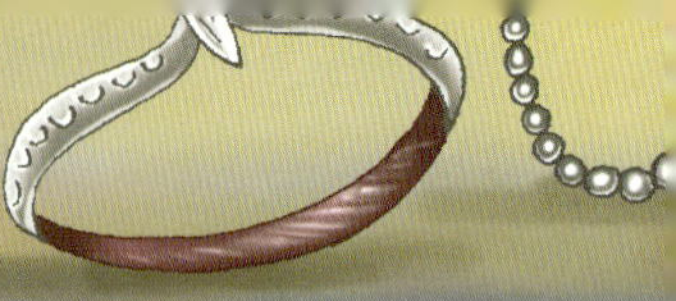

source, consists of 11 per cent hydrogen and 89 per cent oxygen by mass. This macroscopic composition corresponds to the molecular composition, which consists of two hydrogen atoms combined with one oxygen atom. The properties of a compound differ entirely from those of its constituent elements. For example, water is made up of hydrogen and oxygen. However, the properties of hydrogen and oxygen (both gases) are different from water (liquid). Hydrogen is combustible, oxygen is a supporter of combustion and water (made up of both hydrogen and oxygen) puts out a flame! Energy changes are involved in the formation of almost every compound. A compound is a homogenous substance, that is, it has same properties and composition everywhere. All compounds have fixed melting points and boiling points.

Mixtures

Each substance in a mixture retains its own chemical identity and hence its own properties. Whereas pure substances have fixed compositions, the compositions of mixtures can vary. Some mixtures do not have the same composition, properties and appearance throughout the mixture. For example, sand, rocks and wood, etc. Such mixtures are heterogeneous. The mixtures that are uniform throughout are homogeneous. Salt, sugar, and many other substances dissolve in water to form homogeneous mixtures. Homogeneous mixtures are also called **solutions**.

Periodic table

The periodic table is the most important reference for the elements in chemistry. It arranges all the known elements in an informative array. Elements are arranged left to right and top to bottom in order of increasing atomic number. The order generally coincides with increasing atomic mass. The different rows of elements are called periods. The period number of an element signifies the highest energy level an electron in that element occupies. The number of electrons in a period increases as we move down the periodic table. Using the data in the table scientists, students and others who are familiar with the periodic table can extract information concerning individual elements. People also gain information from the periodic table by looking at how it is put together.

Dmitri Mendeleev was the first scientist to create a periodic table of the elements in 1869. This was very similar to the modern periodic table. This showed that when the elements were ordered by increasing atomic weight, a pattern appeared where properties of the elements repeated periodically. This periodic table is a chart that groups the elements according to their similar properties. The most important difference between Mendeleev's table and today's table is that the modern table is organized by increasing atomic number, not increasing atomic weight.

I	II	III	IV	V	VI	VII	VIII		
H 1.01									
Li 6.94	Be 9.01	B 10.8	C 12.0	N 14.0	O 16.0	F 19.0			
Na 23.0	Mg 24.3	Al 27.0	Si 28.1	P 31.0	S 32.1	Cl 35.5			
K 39.1	Ca 40.1		Ti 47.9	V 50.9	Cr 52.0	Mn 54.9	Fe 55.9	Co 58.9	Ni 58.7
Cu 63.5	Zn 65.4			As 74.9	Se 79.0	Br 79.9			
Rb 85.5	Sr 87.6	Y 88.9	Zr 91.2	Nb 92.9	Mo 95.9		Ru 101	Rh 103	Pd 106
Ag 108	Cd 112	In 115	Sn 119	Sb 122	Te 128	I 127			
Ce 133	Ba 137	La 139		Ta 181	W 184		Os 194	Ir 192	Pt 195
Au 197	Hg 201	Ti 204	Pb 207	Bl 209					
			Th 232		U 238				

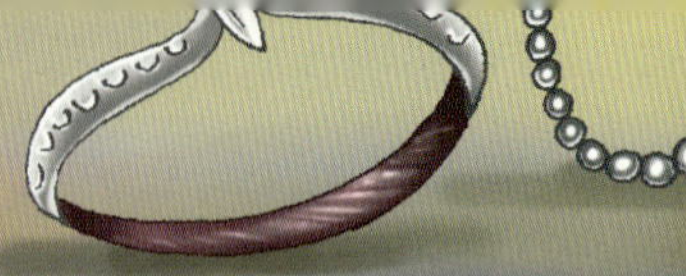

The periodic table helps in predicting some properties of the elements compared to each other. For example, atom size decreases as we move from left to right across the table and increases when we move down a column. Similarly, energy required to remove an electron from an atom increases from left to right and decreases down a column. Elements in the periodic table are arranged in periods and groups. Atomic number increases as we move across a period.

Rows of elements are called periods. The period number of an element signifies the highest unexcited energy level for an electron in that element. The number of elements in a period increases as you move down the periodic table because there are more sublevels per level as the energy level of the atom increases. Columns of periodic table define element groups. Elements within a group share several common properties. Elements in a group have the same outer electron arrangement. The outer electrons are called valence electrons. As they have the same number of **valence electrons**, elements in a group share similar chemical properties. The Roman numerals listed above each group are the usual number of valence electrons. For example, a group VA element will have 5 valence electrons. There are two sets of groups. The group A elements are called the representative elements while the group B elements are called transition elements. Each square on the periodic table gives information about an element's representative symbol, atomic number and atomic weight.

Periodic properties of the elements

If we look carefully at the elements in the periodic table, we will notice that chemical properties of these elements change in a fairly regular fashion. It means that these properties are dependent on the position of the element in the periodic table. As we move from left to right across the periodic table, a number of properties follow a fixed trend. The same thing happens when we move up and down on the periodic table and compare the properties of the elements. Some of the properties that show periodic trends are atomic size, ionization energy, electro-negativity, electron affinity and chemical reactivity.

Above 4°C, water expands when heated and contracts when cooled. But between 4°C and 0°C it does the opposite, contracting when heated and expanding when cooled. Stronger hydrogen and oxygen bonds are formed as the water crystallizes into ice. By the time it's frozen it takes up around 9 per cent more space.

Periodic table of elements

atomic number → 47 | atomic weight → 107.87 | symbol → Ag | name → Silver

- alkali metals
- alkaline earth metals
- transitional metals
- other metals
- nonmetals
- noble gases

1 1.01 **H** Hydrogen																	2 4.003 **He** Helium
3 6.94 **Li** Lithium	4 9.01 **Be** Beryllium											5 10.81 **B** Baron	6 12.01 **C** Carbon	7 14.01 **N** Nitrogen	8 15.999 **O** Oxygen	9 18.998 **F** Fluorine	10 20.18 **Ne** Neon
11 22.99 **Na** Sodium	12 24.31 **Mg** Magnesium											13 26.98 **Al** Alluminum	14 28.09 **Si** Silicon	15 30.97 **P** Phosphorus	16 32.06 **S** Sulfur	17 35.45 **Cl** Chlorine	18 39.95 **Ar** Argon
19 39.10 **K** Potassium	20 40.08 **Ca** Calcium	21 44.96 **Sc** Scandium	22 47.90 **Ti** Titanium	23 50.94 **V** Vanadium	24 51.996 **Cr** Chromium	25 54.94 **Mn** Manganese	26 55.85 **Fe** Iron	27 58.93 **Co** Cobalt	28 58.70 **Ni** Nickel	29 63.55 **Cu** Copper	30 65.37 **Zn** Zinc	31 59.72 **Ga** Gallium	32 72.59 **Ge** Germanium	33 74.92 **As** Arsenic	34 78.96 **Se** Selenium	35 79.90 **Br** Bromine	36 83.80 **Kr** Krypton
37 85.47 **Rb** Rubidium	38 87.62 **Sr** Strontium	39 88.91 **Y** Yttrium	40 91.22 **Zr** Zirconium	41 92.91 **Nb** Niobium	42 95.94 **Mo** Molybdenum	43 (98) **Tc** Technetium	44 101.07 **Ru** Ruthenium	45 102.91 **Rh** Rhodium	46 106.40 **Pd** Palladium	47 107.87 **Ag** Silver	48 112.41 **Cd** Cadmium	49 114.82 **In** Indium	50 118.69 **Sn** Tin	51 121.75 **Sb** Antimony	52 127.60 **Te** Tellurium	53 126.90 **I** Iodine	54 131.30 **Xe** Xenon
55 132.91 **Cs** Cesium	56 137.33 **Ba** Barium	57 138.91 **La** Lanthanum	72 178.49 **Hf** Hafnium	73 180.95 **Ta** Tantalum	74 183.85 **W** Tungsten	75 186.21 **Re** Rhenium	76 190.20 **Os** Osmium	77 192.22 **Ir** Iridium	78 195.09 **Pt** Platinum	79 196.97 **Au** Gold	80 200.59 **Hg** Mercury	81 204.37 **Tl** Thallium	82 207.19 **Pb** Lead	83 208.98 **Bi** Bismuth	84 (209) **Po** Polonium	85 (210) **At** Astatine	86 (222) **Rn** Radon
87 (223) **Fr** Francium	88 226.03 **Ra** Radium	89 227.03 **Ac** Actinium	104 (261) **Rf** Rutherfordium	105 (262) **Ha** Hahnium	106 (266) **Sg** Seaborgium	107 (262) **Bh** Bohrium	108 (265) **Hs** Hassium	109 (266) **Mt** Meitnerium	110 (271)	111 (272)	112 (277)	(113)	114 (285)	(115)	116 (289)	(117)	118 (293)

58 140.12 **Ce** Cerium	59 140.91 **Pr** Praseodymium	60 144.24 **Nd** Neodymium	61 (145) **Pm** Promethium	62 150.40 **Sm** Samarium	63 151.96 **Eu** Europium	64 157.25 **Gd** Gadolinium	65 158.93 **Tb** Terbium	66 162.50 **Dy** Dysprosium	67 164.93 **Ho** Holmium	68 167.26 **Er** Erbium	69 168.93 **Tm** Thulium	70 173.04 **Yb** Ytterbium	71 174.97 **Lu** Lutetium
90 232.04 **Th** Thorium	91 231.04 **Pa** Protactinium	92 238.03 **U** Uranium	93 237.05 **Np** Naptunium	94 (244) **Pu** Plutonium	95 (243) **Am** Americium	96 (247) **Cm** Curium	97 (247) **Bk** Berkelium	98 (251) **Cf** Californium	99 (252) **Es** Einsteinium	100 (257) **Fm** Fermium	101 (260) **Md** Mendelevium	102 (259) **No** Nobelium	103 (262) **Lr** Lawrencium

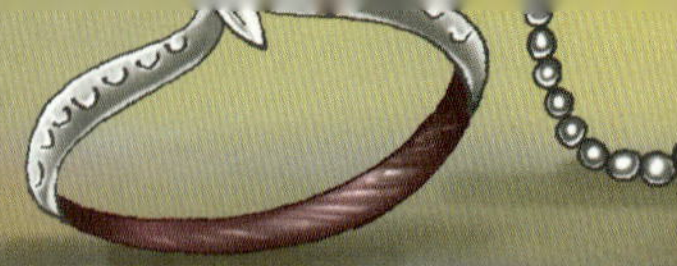

Atomic radius

The atomic radius of an element is half of the distance between the centres of two atoms of that element that are just touching each other. Generally, the atomic radius decreases across a period from left to right and increases while moving down a group. The atoms with the largest atomic radii are located in Group I and at the bottom of groups.

Moving from left to right across a period, electrons are added one at a time to the outer energy shell. Electrons within a shell cannot shield each other from the attraction to protons. Since the number of protons is also increasing, the effective nuclear charge increases across a period. This causes the atomic radius to decrease.

Moving down a group in the periodic table, the number of electrons and filled electron shells increases, but the number of valence electrons remains the same. The outermost electrons in a group are exposed to the same effective nuclear charge, but electrons are found farther from the nucleus as the number of filled energy shells increases. Therefore, the atomic radii increase.

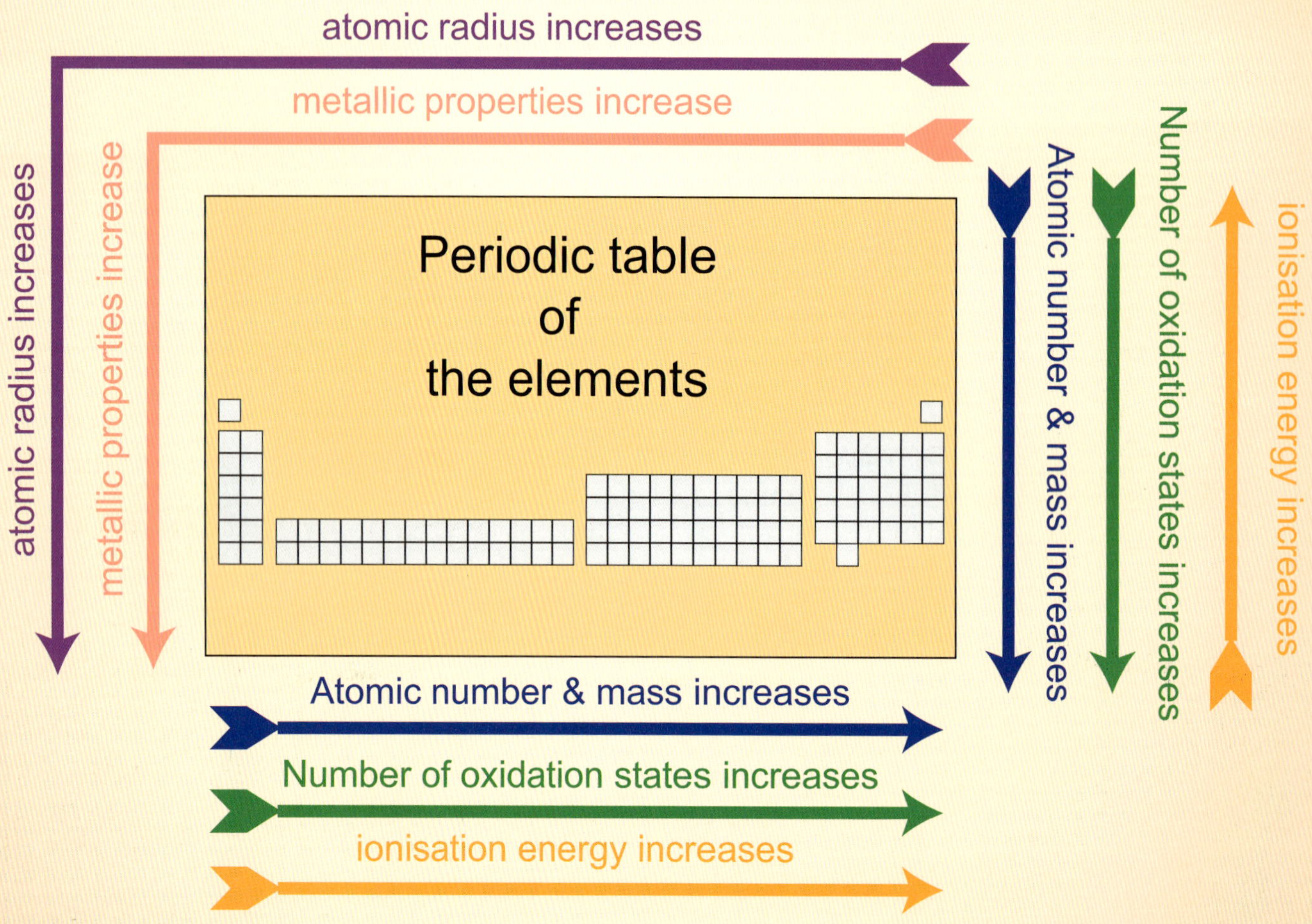

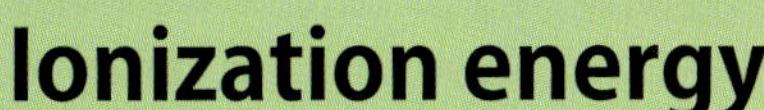

Ionization energy

The ionization energy is defined as the energy required for completely removing an electron from a gaseous atom or ion. The closer and more tightly bound an electron is to the nucleus, the more difficult it will be to remove, and the higher its ionization energy will be. The first ionization energy is the energy required to remove one electron from the parent atom. The second ionization energy is the energy required to remove a second valence electron from the univalent ion to form the divalent ion, and so on. Successive ionization energies increase. The second ionization energy is always greater than the first ionization energy. Ionization energies increase moving from left to right across a period (decreasing atomic radius). Ionization energy decreases moving down a group (increasing atomic radius). Group I elements have low ionization energies because the loss of an electron forms a stable octet.

Electron affinity

Electron affinity of an element can be defined as the ability of an atom to accept an electron. Atoms with stronger effective nuclear charge have greater electron affinity. Some generalizations can be made about the electron affinities of certain groups in the periodic table. The Group IIA elements, commonly known as the alkaline earths, have low electron affinities. Group VIIA elements, the halogens, have high electron affinities because the addition of an electron to an atom results in a completely filled shell. Group VIII elements, noble gases, have electron affinities very near to zero. This is due to the fact that each atom of noble gases possesses a stable octet and does not accept an electron readily. Elements of other groups have low electron affinities.

Electro-negativity

Electro-negativity is defined as the measure of the attraction of an atom for the electrons in a chemical bond. The higher electro-negativity of an atom means that it has greater attraction for bonding electrons. This property of an atom is related to ionization energy. Electrons with low ionization energies have low electro-negativities because their nuclei do not exert a strong attractive force on electrons. Similarly, elements with high ionization energies have high electro-negativities due to the strong pull exerted on electrons by their nucleus. In a group, the electro-negativity decreases as atomic number increases. This is because the distance between the valence electrons and nucleus increases.

$+ e^{-} \rightarrow$

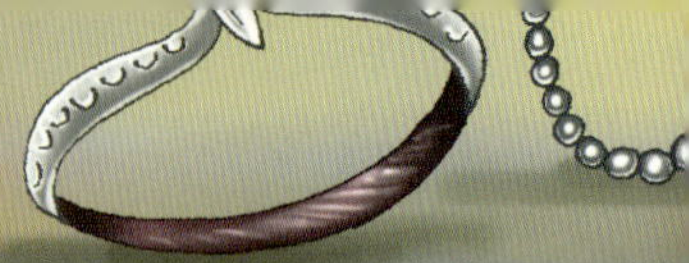

Element groups

All the elements in a periodic table are classified according to their properties. The major categories of elements are described as the following:

1. **Metals:** Most elements are metals. They are located on the left side and the middle of the periodic table. Group IA and Group IIA are the most active metals and they are known as **alkali metals**. The transition elements, groups IB to VIIIB, are also metals. Most of the metals are shiny solids at room temperature but mercury is the exception. They have high melting points and densities. They are characterized by large atomic radius, low ionization energy and low electro-negativity. These properties are due to the fact that the electrons in the valence shell of a metal atom can be removed easily. One important characteristic of metals is their ability to be deformed without breaking. So, they are malleable and ductile. Malleability is the ability of a metal to be hammered into shapes and ductility is the ability of a metal to be drawn into wire. As the valence electrons can move freely, metals are good heat and electricity conductors.

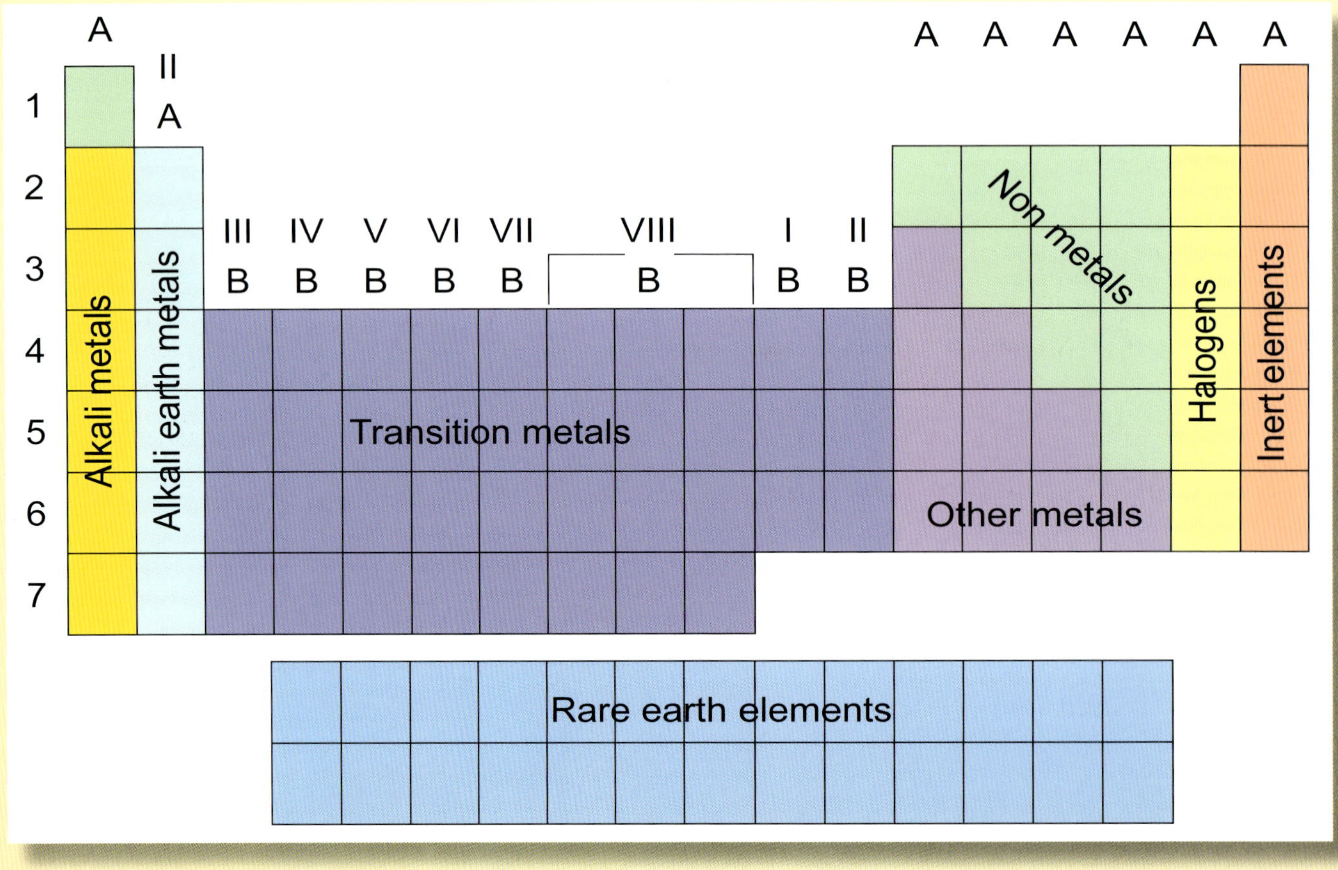

2. **Non-metals:** The non-metals are located on the upper right side of the periodic table. Non-metals are separated from metals by a line that cuts diagonally through the region of the periodic table. Non-metals have high ionization energies and electro-negativities. Solid non-metals are brittle. They have little or no metallic lustre. Most non-metals have the ability to gain electrons easily. Non-metals display a wide range of chemical properties and reactivity. They are generally poor conductors of heat and electricity.

3. **Noble Gases:** The noble gases, also known as the inert gases, are located in Group VIII of the periodic table. The noble gases are relatively nonreactive. This is because they have a complete valence shell. They have little tendency to gain or lose electrons. The noble gases have high ionization energies and negligible electro-negativities. The noble gases have low boiling points and are all gases at room temperature.

24 .003 He Helium
10 20.18 Ne Neon
18 39.95 Ar Argon
36 83.80 Kr Krypton
54 131.30 Xe Xenon
86 (222) Rn Radon

4. **Halogens:** The halogens are located in Group VIIA of the periodic table. The halogens are also considered reactive non-metals. They have seven valence electrons. The main halogen elements are fluorine, chlorine, bromine, iodine. As a group, halogens exhibit highly variable physical properties. Halogens exist in all forms of matter at room temperature, such that solid (iodine), liquid (bromine) and gas (fluorine and chlorine). The chemical properties of halogens are more uniform. The halogens have very high electro-negativities. Fluorine has the highest electro-negativity of all elements. The halogens are particularly reactive with the alkali metals and alkaline earths and form stable ionic crystals.

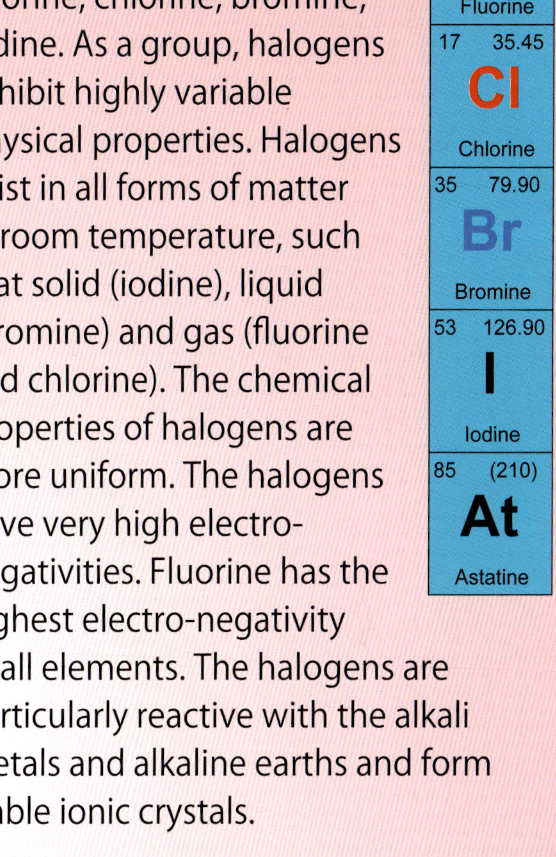

Arsenic is a highly poisonous metallic element having three allotropic forms, yellow, black, and gray. Out of them brittle and crystalline gray form is the most common. Arsenic and its compounds are used in insecticides, weed killers, solid-state doping agents and various alloys. The name originates from Greek word 'arsenikos'.

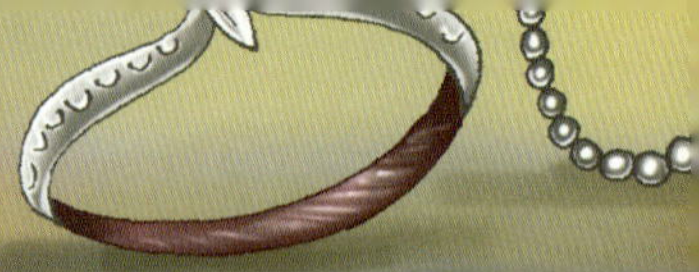

5. **Metalloids:** The metalloids, also known as semimetals, are located along the line between the metals and non-metals in the periodic table. The metalloids are boron, silicon, germanium, arsenic, antimony, and tellurium. The electro-negativities and ionization energies of the metalloids are between those of the metals and non-metals, so the metalloids exhibit characteristics of both classes. For example, silicon possesses a metallic lustre but it is brittle and a poor conductor. The reactivity of the metalloids depends on the elements with which they are reacting. For example, when boron reacts with sodium, it acts as a non-metal while it acts as a metal when reacting with fluorine. The boiling points, melting points and densities of the metalloids vary widely. The intermediate conductivity of metalloids provides them the tendency to make good semiconductors.

6. **Alkali Metals:** The alkali metals are the elements located in Group IA of the periodic table. The alkali metals are lithium, sodium, potassium, rubidium, caesium and francium. The alkali metals exhibit many of the physical properties common to metals but their densities are lower than those of common metals. They have one electron in their outer shell, which is loosely bound. Due to this, they have the largest atomic radii of the elements in their respective periods. An alkali metal can easily lose its valence electron to form the univalent cation. Their low ionization energies result in their metallic properties and high reactivity. Alkali metals have low electro-negativities. They react readily with non-metals, especially halogens.

1 H 1.008																	2 He 4.003
3 Li 6.941	4 Be 9.012											5 B 10.81	6 C 12.01	7 N 14.01	8 O 16.00	9 F 19.00	10 Ne 20.18
11 Na 22.99	12 Mg 24.31											13 Al 26.98	14 Si 28.09	15 P 30.97	16 S 32.07	17 Cl 35.45	18 Ar 39.95
19 K 39.10	20 Ca 40.08	21 Sc 44.96	22 Ti 47.88	23 Y 50.94	24 Cr 52.00	25 Mn 54.94	26 Fe 55.85	27 Co 58.47	28 Ni 58.69	29 Cu 63.55	30 Zn 65.39	31 Ga 69.72	32 Ge 72.59	33 As 74.92	34 Se 78.96	35 Br 79.90	36 Kr 83.80
37 Rb 85.47	38 Sr 87.62	39 Y 88.91	40 Zr 91.22	41 Nb 92.91	42 Mo 95.94	43 Tc (98)	44 Ru 101.1	45 Rh 102.9	46 Pd 106.4	47 Ag 107.9	48 Cd 112.4	49 In 114.8	50 Sn 118.7	51 Sb 121.8	52 Tc 127.6	53 I 126.9	54 Xe 131.3
55 Cs 132.9	56 Ba 137.3	*	72 Hf 178.5	73 Ta 180.9	74 W 183.9	75 Re 186.2	76 Os 190.2	77 Ir 190.2	78 Pr 195.1	79 Au 197.0	80 Hg 200.5	81 Tl 204.4	82 Pb 207.2	83 Bi 209.0	84 Po (209)	85 At (210)	86 Rn (222)
87 Fr (223)	88 Ra (226)	**	104 Rf (261)	105 Db (262)	106 Sg (266)	107 Bh (264)	108 Hs (269)	109 Mt (268)	110 Ds (291)	111 Rg (272)	112 Uub (285)	113 Uut (284)	114 Uuq (289)	115 Uup (288)	116 Uuh (292)	117 Uus 0	118 Uuo (294)

7. **Alkaline Earths:** The alkaline earths consist of the elements located in Group IIA of the periodic table. They possess many of the characteristic properties of metals. They have low electron affinities and low electro-negativities. Similar to the alkali metals, the properties of alkaline earths depend on the ease with which electrons are lost. They have two electrons in their outer shell. So, they have smaller atomic radii than the alkali metals. The two valence electrons are not tightly bound to the nucleus which makes them to lose the electrons to form divalent cations.

8. **Transition Metals:** The transition elements are located in groups IB to VIIIB of the periodic table. Due to the fact that they possess the properties of metals, they are also known as the transition metals. These elements are very hard. They have high melting points and boiling points. The electrons in the last orbital (d orbital) are loosely bound, which contributes to the high electrical conductivity and malleability of the transition elements. They have low ionization energies. They exhibit a wide range of oxidation states or positively charged forms. The positive oxidation states allow transition elements to form many different ionic compounds. Their complexes form characteristic coloured solutions and compounds. Complex formation reactions sometimes enhance the low solubility of some compounds.

9. **Rare Earths:** There is a block of two rows of elements located at the bottom of the periodic table (6th (5*d* electronic configuration) and 7th (5*f* electronic configuration) periods). The elements in these rows, lanthanum (element 57) and actinium (element 89) are collectively known as the rare earth elements. In true meaning, they aren't particularly rare. They were named so because prior to 1945, long and tedious processes were required to purify these metals from their oxides. The rare earths are silver, silvery-white or gray metals. They have a high lustre but tarnish readily in air. They have high electrical conductivity. The rare earths share many common properties. This makes them difficult to separate or even distinguish from each other. There are very small differences in solubility and complex formation between them. The rare earth metals naturally occur together in minerals. Most of their compounds are strongly paramagnetic.

Lanthanide series	58 **Ce** 140.12	59 **Pr** 140.91	60 **Nd** 144.24	61 **Pm** 146.92°	62 **Sm** 150.36	63 **Eu** 151.96	64 **Gd** 157.25	65 **Tb** 158.93	66 **Dy** 162.50	67 **Ho** 164.93	68 **Er** 167.26	69 **Tm** 168.93	70 **Yb** 173.04	71 **Lu** 174.97
Actinide series	90 **Th** 232.04°	91 **Pa** 231.04°	92 **U** 238.03	93 **Np** 237.05°	94 **Pu** 239.05°	95 **Am** 241.06°	96 **Cm** 244.06°	97 **Bk** 249.08°	98 **Cf** 252.08°	99 **Es** 252.08°	100 **Fm** 257.10°	101 **Md** 258.10°	102 **No** 259.10°	103 **Lr** 262.11°

Lanthanides

The lanthanides are metals that are located in block 5d of the periodic table. The lanthanides are not as rare as were once thought. Even the scarce rare earths (e.g., europium, lutetium) are more common than the platinum-group metals. Several lanthanides form during the fission of uranium and plutonium. The lanthanides have many scientific and industrial uses. Their compounds are used as catalysts in the production of petroleum and synthetic products. Lanthanides are used in lamps, lasers, magnets, phosphors, motion picture projectors and X-ray intensifying screens.

The lanthanides are silvery-white metals that tarnish when exposed to air, forming their oxides. They are relatively soft metals but hardness increases with higher atomic number. Moving from left to right across the period (increasing atomic number), the radius of each lanthanide ion decreases. This is known as 'lanthanide contraction'. They have high melting points and boiling points. They are very reactive and burn easily in air. At elevated temperatures, many rare earths ignite and burn vigorously. They are strong reducing agents.

Actinides

The actinides are f block elements. So, their electronic configurations utilize the f sublevel. All of them are dense radioactive metals that are highly electropositive. They tarnish readily in air and combine with most non-metals. They are very dense metals with distinctive structures. They react with boiling water or dilute acid to release hydrogen gas. They combine directly with most non-metals. As of today, a prime area of application of actinides units is the production of nuclear energy. Study of the properties of the actinides is hampered by their radioactive instability. It is known, however, that all members of the series resemble each other in their chemical properties. Also, they have a strong chemical resemblance to their homolog elements in the lanthanide series. The actinides are reactive and possess a number of different valences in their compounds.

Helium is a colourless, odourless, inert gaseous element constituting approximately one per cent of Earth's atmosphere, from which it is commercially obtained by fractionation. It is commonly used in electric light bulbs, fluorescent tubes, and radio vacuum tubes and as an inert gas shield in arc welding. The name originates from the Greek word 'helios' meaning the sun.

Chemical compounds

A substance containing atoms of more than one element in a definite ratio is called a compound. The composition of a compound is represented by its chemical formula. In the chemical reaction of carbon and oxygen to form carbon dioxide, the elements are in a definite ratio 1:2. Here, one atom of carbon combines with two atoms of oxygen and forms the compound carbon dioxide (CO_2). When several atoms are so tightly bonded together that they physically behave as a unit, the unit is called a molecule. Elements and compounds can be molecular. In the carbon dioxide reaction, the O_2 molecule contains 2 oxygen atoms and CO_2 molecule contains 3 atoms—1 carbon and 2 oxygen.

C	+	O_2	→	CO_2
One atom		two atoms		three atoms

A compound is a pure substance consisting of two (or more) elements that are chemically bonded in a fixed proportion. Unlike a mixture, in which components retain their characteristics, a compound is a new entity. For example, atoms of oxygen and hydrogen can be mixed in any proportion and resulting mixture will contain hydrogen molecules and oxygen molecules. Water, however, is a compound of oxygen and hydrogen because its molecules combine both elements in a fixed proportion, as expressed by the formula H_2O.

Certain elements can combine with each other in more than one proportion. For example, carbon monoxide and carbon dioxide both contain carbon and oxygen. A molecule of carbon monoxide (CO) consists of one carbon atom and one oxygen atom. In carbon dioxide (CO_2), one carbon atom is bonded with two oxygen atoms to form a molecule of the compound. These two compounds are quite different.

Covalent and ionic compounds

According to the type of bond with which its atoms are held, a compound can be either covalent or ionic. A covalent compound is held together by covalent bonds. A covalent bond holds two atoms together to create diatomic molecules, such as O_2 and N_2. The major covalent compounds include water, carbon monoxide and carbon dioxide. An ionic compound contains charged ions -cations (positively charged ions) and anions (negatively charged ions). Sodium chloride is a typical ionic compound which has an equal number of sodium ions and chlorine ions. A sodium cation (Na^+) is created when a sodium atom loses an electron; a chlorine anion (Cl^-) is created when a chlorine atom gains an electron. In an ionic compound, the ions are held together by the ionic bond. An ionic bond can be

defined as the attraction between the positively charged ion and its negatively charged counterpart.

Organic and inorganic compounds

Compounds can also be divided into organic and inorganic. Organic compounds contain carbon atoms. Examples of organic compounds are methane (CH_4), a small hydrocarbon compound, and large polymers, which include proteins, carbohydrates, and nucleic acids. Inorganic compounds, which include water and many minerals, usually contain elements other than carbon. Examples of inorganic compounds are water and minerals (with some exceptions).

Co-ordination compounds

Co-ordination compounds are different from acids, bases and salts because of their method of bonding. Acids, bases and salts are formed when atoms give or take electrons to form ionic bonds, share pairs of electrons to form covalent bonds or exchange electrons in some fashion intermediary between these cases to form polar covalent bonds. Coordination compounds, on the other hand, are formed when one or more ions or molecules contribute both electrons in a bonding pair to a metallic atom or ion. The contributing species in such a compound is known as ligand. There is a group of compounds which combines an organic and an inorganic substance together. Because the inorganic component is usually a metal, these compounds are called organometallics. Examples are chlorophyll, haemoglobin and vitamin B_{12}.

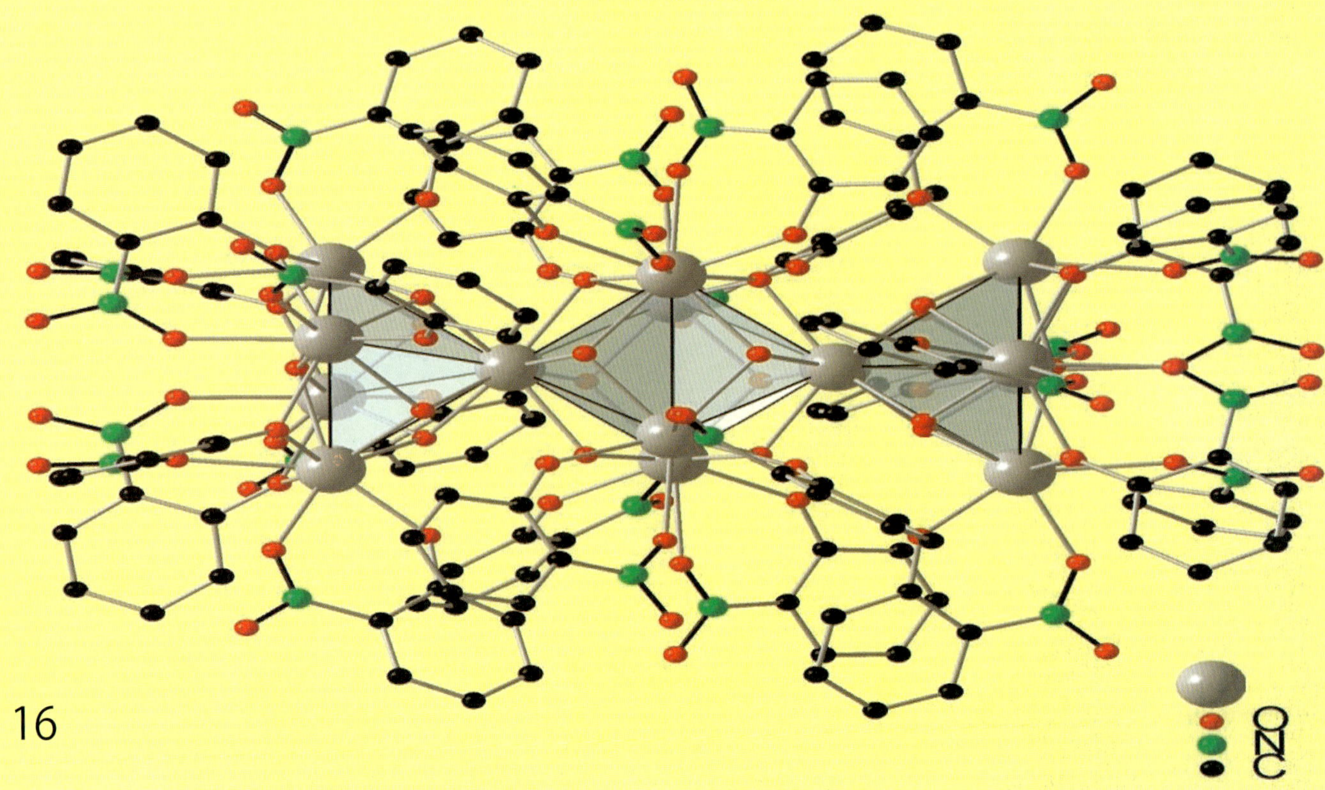

Some important elements

Hydrogen

H[1]
1

Hydrogen was first recognized as a gaseous substance in 1766 by English chemist and physicist Henry Cavendish. The abundance of hydrogen in the Earth's crust is 1,520 parts per million. Hydrogen is the major constituent of the universe. Under ordinary conditions, hydrogen is a colourless, odourless, tasteless gas that is only slightly soluble in water. It is the least dense gas known. Ordinary hydrogen gas exists as a diatomic molecule (H_2). It reacts with oxygen to form its major compound on Earth, water (H_2O). It reacts with nitrogen, halogens and sulfur, to form ammonia (NH_3), hydrogen chloride (HCl) and hydrogen sulfide (H_2S), respectively. It combines with several metals to form metal hydrides, and carbon to form many organic compounds.

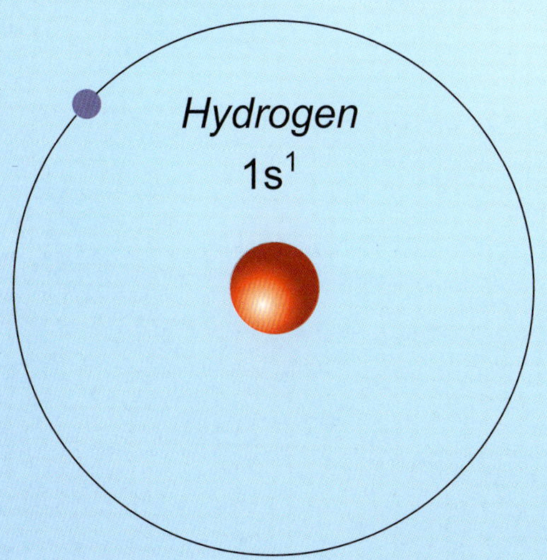

Hydrogen is a mixture of three isotopes—protium, deuterium, and tritium. The fusion of protium nuclei (protons) to form helium is believed to be the major source of the sun's energy. The extreme heat of reaction in hydrogen-oxygen burning is used in high temperature welding and melting processes. Hydrogen molecule addition reaction is commonly known as hydrogenation. These reactions are widely used in industry for the hardening of animal fats or vegetable oils, for the synthesis of methanol from carbon monoxide and in petroleum refining.

Bromine is a heavy, volatile, corrosive, reddish-brown and non-metallic liquid element. Another liquid element in periodic table is mercury. It has a highly irritating vapour. The most common uses of Bromine are in Gasoline anti-knock mixtures, Fumigants, Poisons, Dyes, Photographic chemicals, Medicines and brominated vegetable oil. Its name is originated from the Greek word 'Bromos' meaning "stench".

Carbon

C	6
12.01	

Carbon is the sixth most abundant element in the universe and possibly the most widespread element on Earth. It is named from the Latin word *carbo*, meaning charcoal. It has been known since ancient times and is found in all living things. This is a very important constituent of the atmosphere— carbon dioxide. In its elemental form, carbon can be found as diamond, the hardest naturally occurring substance; graphite, an excellent lubricant or as a fullerene. Although five isotopes of carbon are known, only C-12 and C-13 are stable. The presence of trace amounts of C-14, a radioactive isotope is used in 'carbon dating' of historical objects.

Carbon is unique among the elements as carbon atoms can form bonds with other carbon atoms. This property is known as **catenation**. The carbon containing compounds are commonly termed as organic compounds. There are more than several million known organic compounds. Carbon is a major constituent of most of our fuels—natural gas, petroleum, coal, wood and other biomass. Carbon is a major constituent of most polymers, both naturally occurring ones such as cellulose, starch, ribonucleic acid (RNA) , deoxyribonucleic acid (DNA), silk, and wool, as well as synthetic ones, including nylon, Teflon, polyethylene and polystyrene. Some of the strongest and most modern materials replacing metals are made of carbon fibers.

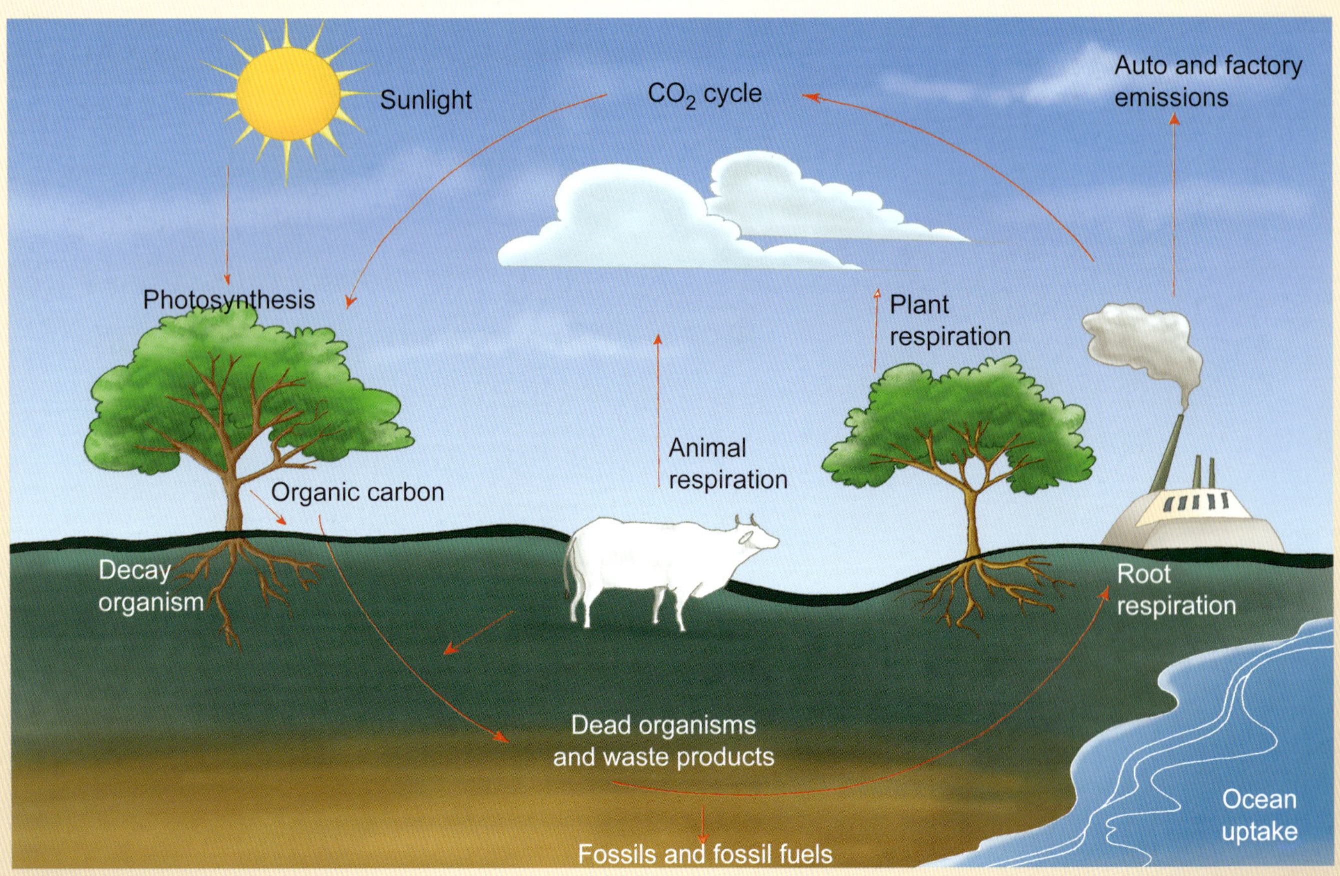

Nitrogen

7
N
14.01

Nitrogen is a gaseous element that is abundant in the atmosphere. Scottish chemist Daniel Rutherford, Swedish chemist Carl Wilhelm Scheele and English chemist Henry Cavendish independently discovered nitrogen in 1772. In 1790, French chemist Jean-Antoine Chaptal coined the term nitrogen after realizing that it was present in nitrate (NO_3-) and nitric acid (HNO_3). Nitrogen is the most abundant terrestrial element in an uncombined state and it makes up 78 per cent of Earth's atmosphere. Nitrogen is essential for life because it is a constituent of the nucleotides of DNA and RNA molecules that encode genetic information.

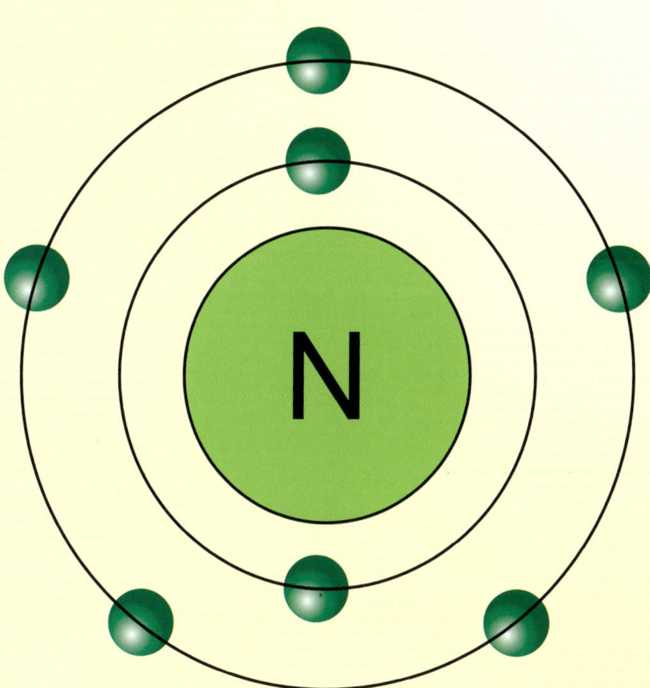

Nitrogen molecule (N_2) possesses the strongest known chemical bond and its bond dissociation energy is 945 kJ mol^{-1}. This colourless, tasteless, odourless gas is relatively non-reactive because of its strong N-N triple bond and stable electronic configuration. Liquid nitrogen is used as a refrigerant in the laboratory and food industry and in the preservation of biological samples. The major industrial applications of nitrogen-containing compounds are in fertilizers and explosives. The most important nitrogenous compound is ammonia (NH_3). Ammonia is used as a fertilizer, refrigerant, non-aqueous solvent and precursor for many nitrogen compounds including nylon and plastics. Other important nitrogen compounds are nitric acid (HNO_3), ammonium nitrate (NH_4NO_3) and urea ($H_2NC[O]NH_2$). Nitrous oxide (N_2O) is used as a dental anesthetic and aerosol propellant. Nitric oxide (NO) is the simplest stable odd-electron molecule and a short-lived, biologically active neurotransmitter (chemicals which transmit signals from a neuron to a target cell), cytotoxic agent (toxic to cells) in immunology, and major component along with NO_2 in acid rain and smog. The strong reducing agent hydrazine (N_2H_4) is another important nitrogen compound which is used in rocket fuels.

Oxygen

8
O
15.99

British chemist Joseph Priestley and the Swedish chemist Carl Wilhelm Scheele are credited for the discovery of oxygen by isolating oxygen in the gaseous state. Scheele was the first scientist who discovered oxygen in 1771 but it was Priestley who discovered oxygen in 1774 and proved that oxygen was essential to combustion and respiration. He published his findings in the same year and called the new gas 'dephlogisticated air'. The name 'oxygen' was coined by a French chemist, Antoine Lavoisier in 1775. He was the first scientist who recognized oxygen as an element, characterized it and described its role in combustion.

A life on Earth cannot be imagined without oxygen. Animals and plants require it for respiration and to survive. It is tasteless, colourless and odourless gaseous element that is only slightly soluble in water. It is the third most abundant element of the universe. It constitutes almost 21 per cent of the Earth's atmosphere and half of the Earth's crust. Oxygen is commonly used in oxidizers, rocket propulsion, medicines, welding, sensors, oxygen masks and concentrators. Oxygen is very reactive. Its reaction with another substance to form an oxide is called oxidation. It is a constituent of a number of compound groups, such as acids, hydroxides, carbonates, chlorates, nitrates and nitrites, and phosphates. It is also a constituent of organic compounds such as carbohydrates, proteins, fats and oils.

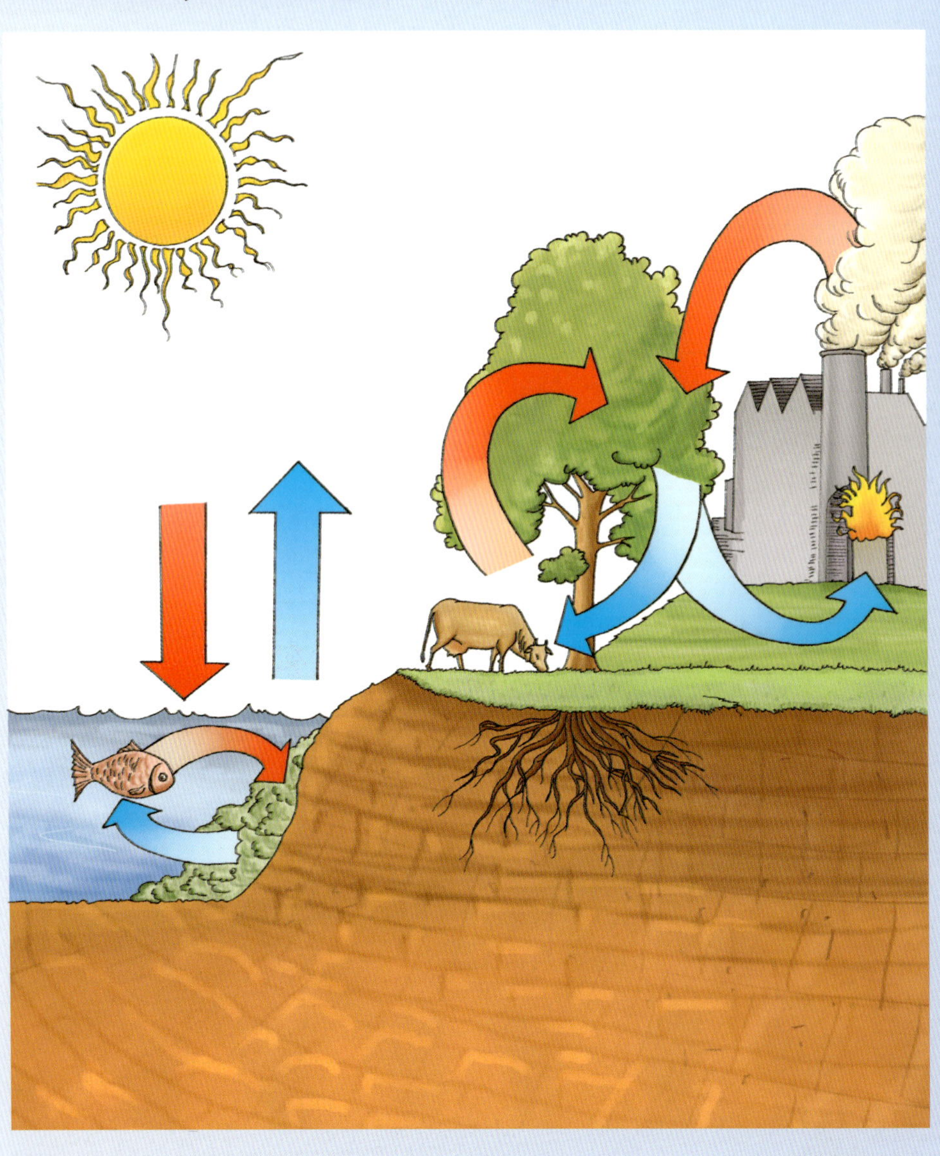

Sodium

11
Na
22.99

Sodium is a soft, silvery alkali metal and reacts vigorously with water to generate hydrogen gas. The name sodium is derived from a Medieval Latin name for a headache remedy 'sodanum'. Humphry Davy isolated the element in 1807 by the electrolysis of caustic soda (NaOH). Water and sodium acetate mixing causes a hot pack to release heat. Hot packs are used to relieve stiffness and pain. Though sodium compounds are quite common in nature but sodium is never found in its elemental form. Sodium is the most abundant alkali metal and the seventh most abundant element in Earth's crust. Sodium burns yellow-orange in the flame test.

Its primary use had been as a substance used in the production of tetraethyl lead, an anti-knocking gasoline additive. An alloy of sodium and potassium is used in nuclear reactors as a heat transfer agent. Appropriate sodium ion levels (along with potassium levels) are essential for proper cell function in biological systems.

Several sodium compounds are economically important. Sodium chloride (NaCl) is common salt which is a de-icing compound, a condiment and a food preservative. Sodium hydroxide (NaOH) is used in the manufacture of soaps, detergents, and cleansers. Na_2CO_3 (washing soda) is used to make glass, soaps, fire extinguishers and 'scrubbers' that remove SO_2 from gases generated in power plants. The paper industry uses Na2SO4 (salt cake) to make brown wrapping paper and corrugated boxes.

Beryllium is a lightweight, corrosion-resistant, rigid and steel-gray metallic element. It has very high melting point. It is used as an aerospace structural material and as a moderator and reflector in nuclear reactors. It is also used in a copper alloy which is used for springs, electrical contacts and non-sparking tools.

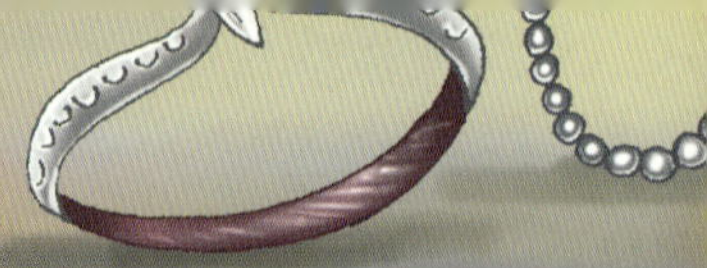

Aluminium

Aluminium is a silvery-white metallic element. It was discovered in 1825 by Danish chemist Hans Christian Orsted. It is the most abundant metal found in Earth's crust, comprising 8.3 per cent of the crust's total weight. Aluminium is not found in its metallic state in nature. It is usually found as silicate, oxide or hydrated oxide (bauxite). Its extraction from ore is difficult and expensive. So, it is generally recycled because the energy required for recycling is only 5 per cent of the energy needed to extract the metal.

Aluminium is lightweight, ductile and easily machined. It is protected by an oxide film from reacting with air and water, and is therefore rust-resistant. It is one of the lightest metals but is quite tough. So, it is the most useful in metallurgy and transportation (for example, aircraft, automobiles, railroad cars and boats). It is regularly used for manufacturing window frames and decorative ornaments. It is also used in the manufacture of cooking gear as it is a good conductor of heat. Aluminium foils are a household convenience for protecting food from spoiling and providing insulation. Aluminium-made beverage cans are widely manufactured for variety of purposes. The average human body contains about 35 milligrams of aluminium.

Hot peppers get their heat from a molecule called capsaicin. While the molecule acts as an irritant to mammals, including humans, birds lack the receptor responsible for the effect and are immune to the burning sensation from exposure.

Chlorine

17
Cl
35.45

Chlorine is one of the elements of the halogen family. It was the first halogen to be discovered. In 1774, a Swedish chemist Carl Wilhelm Scheele, produced chlorine by the reaction of manganese dioxide (MnO_2) with a solution of hydrochloric acid (HCl). In 1810, an English chemist Sir Humphry Davy, determined chlorine as an element. He also named it chlorine, the word being derived from the Greek word *chloros* meaning 'pale green'. Chlorine is toxic in nature. It has a high electro-negativity that is about equal to that of oxygen.

Chlorine is the most abundant of the halogens. It is produced commercially by electrolysis of seawater and brines. The most common compound of chlorine is Sodium chloride (NaCl) or common table salt. It can be obtained from seaside evaporation pools or mined from underground deposits. Chlorine and its compounds have a large number of everyday uses. Chlorine is used in water purification as well in the production of safe plumbing components constructed of polyvinyl chloride (PVC). Chlorinated dyes, medicines, pesticides, disinfectants, and solvents have widespread applications. Chlorofluorocarbon compounds, compounds consisting of chlorine, fluorine and carbon, were widely used as refrigerants, solvents, foaming agents and spray-can propellants. These compounds are now banned by international agreement due to the role of those compounds in the depletion of Earth's protective ozone layer. Chlorine was used during World War I (1914–1918) as a chemical warfare agent.

The only elements that are liquid at room temperature are bromine and mercury. However, you can melt gallium by holding a lump in the warmth of your hand.

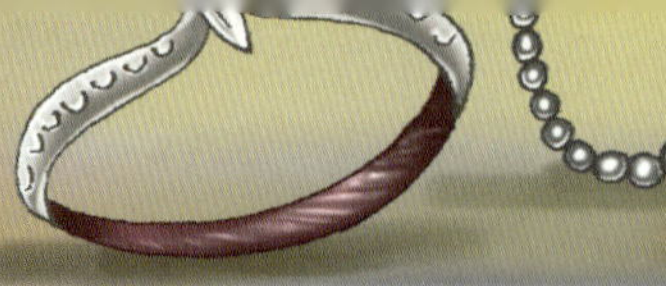

Iron

Iron is the major element in the Earth's core. It is the fourth most abundant element in the Earth's crust. In the crust, iron is found mainly as the oxide minerals hematite (Fe_2O_3) and magnetite (Fe_3O_4). Iron is an essential element in almost all living organisms. Iron has a very stable nucleus and has fourteen known isotopes. Pure iron is a soft, white and lustrous metal. It oxidizes in moist air but is stable in dry air. The oxidation of iron in the presence of moisture causes rusting. Fine iron is pyrophoric in nature. Iron dissolves in dilute mineral acid and in hot sodium hydroxide solution.

Iron is one of the most important mineral required by the human body. The main functions of iron include transportation of oxygen and execution of various metabolic processes. Iron is a component of haemoglobin present in the red blood cells. Low iron levels in the body will result in an iron deficiency disease called anaemia. One of the most important uses of iron is in the manufacture of steel. It is also used in the bodies or frames of heavy carriers like ships and heavy vehicles and heavy machinery. It is widely used for making household things like decorative iron fencing, arbors, trellis, furniture and so on.With mild heating, iron reacts with the halogens, sulphur, phosphorus, boron, carbon, and silicon to form a variety of compounds.

Zinc

30
Zn
65.41

Like many transition metals, zinc has been known in impure form since ancient times. Brass (copper and zinc) coins were used by Egyptians and Palestinians in ancient times. Although the origin of the name is unknown, it has been suggested that it is derived from the German word Zincke, meaning 'spike' or 'tooth'.

Zinc is a trace element in Earth's crust. Pure zinc is a silver-white solid at room temperature. Like other metals, zinc conducts electricity and can be transformed into wires or sheets for various purposes. Some properties of zinc are quite different from those of the other transition metals, for example, it has relatively low melting point, boiling point and density. These different properties are attributed because of the filled outermost sub-shell of electrons. This also causes it to be relatively unreactive. It is found predominantly as a sulphide compound (ZnS).

Due to the low reactivity of zinc, its most common use is in anticorrosion coatings. Zinc is also often used to form alloys. The most common alloys of zinc include brass and commercial bronze. Pennies minted after 1983 are made of a core of zinc surrounded by copper. Historically, zinc was used by Alessandro Volta to produce the first battery. Zinc ions, due to their low reactivity, have important biological roles.

In animals, it is the most abundant metallic cofactor (a metal bound to an enzyme and required for its biological activity). It is used by insulin in the regulation of glucose consumption and by hydrolytic enzymes.

Antimony is a metallic element which has four allotropic forms, the most common of which is a hard, extremely brittle, lustrous, silver-white, crystalline material. It is used in a wide variety of alloys, especially with lead in battery plates, and in the manufacture of flame-proofing compounds, paint, semiconductor devices and ceramic products. The name originates from the Greek words 'anti' and 'monos' meaning "opposed to solitude".

Silver

47
Ag
107.87

Silver is a precious metal like gold. The date of its discovery is not known, but it has been identified in jewellery, coins and religious ornaments since ancient civilizations. Silver is the sixty-third most abundant metal in the Earth's crust. It is found naturally as native metal or in ores in which it is complexed with lead, copper, tellurium, mercury or antimony. Its extraction is done by amalgamation and displacement using mercury and smelting methods.

The chemistry of silver was not well-known before 1980, although silver nitrate was used medicinally in the 1800s. Silver is highly reactive in nature due to its ability to form numerous inorganic and organic complexes (halide, sulfide, nitrate, oxide, and acetylide compounds, cyano-derivatives, olefin complexes etc.). Silver compounds are brightly coloured. Silver is used in the manufacture of photographic film chemicals such as silver nitrate. It is used as an analytic reagent in organic chemistry, as a catalyst in photo-oxidation and electrochemical reactions. Silver is also used in the manufacture of bone prostheses, cardiac implants and needles used in ocular surgery. Silver is also used in the making of dental amalgam fillings. It is toxic in nature, so it is used as antiseptic ingredient in silver nitrate, silver sulfadiazine and cerium nitrate. A new generation of sustained silver release products is showing promise in the treatment of skin wounds, skin ulcers, and burns. Activated silver ion is toxic to bacteria and yeasts.

Iodine

53
I
126.9

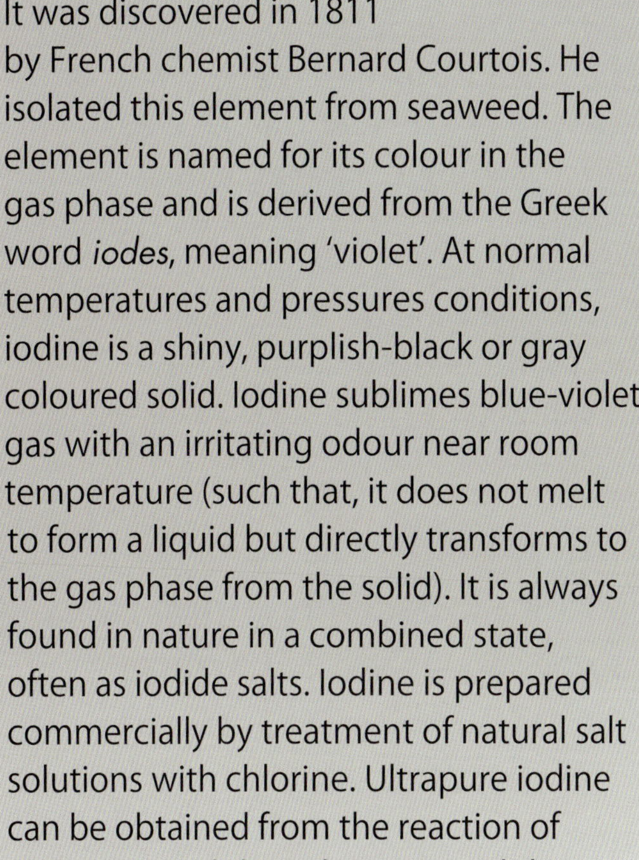

Iodine is the heaviest of the halogen family of elements. It was discovered in 1811 by French chemist Bernard Courtois. He isolated this element from seaweed. The element is named for its colour in the gas phase and is derived from the Greek word *iodes*, meaning 'violet'. At normal temperatures and pressures conditions, iodine is a shiny, purplish-black or gray coloured solid. Iodine sublimes blue-violet gas with an irritating odour near room temperature (such that, it does not melt to form a liquid but directly transforms to the gas phase from the solid). It is always found in nature in a combined state, often as iodide salts. Iodine is prepared commercially by treatment of natural salt solutions with chlorine. Ultrapure iodine can be obtained from the reaction of potassium iodide with copper sulphate.

It forms compounds with many elements, but is less active than the other halogens, which displace it from iodides. Iodine exhibits some metallic-like properties. It dissolves readily in chloroform, carbon tetrachloride or carbon disulfide to form beautiful purple solutions. It is only slightly soluble in water. Iodine is necessary for the proper functioning of the thyroid gland in humans. Dietary deficiencies can be avoided by the occasional consumption of seafood or by using iodized salt, which combines common table salt (NaCl) with potassium iodide (KI). Iodine is a useful antiseptic, either as tincture of iodine (an alcohol solution of iodine) or as an aqueous solution of providone iodine (Betadine). Potassium iodide is also used in photography elements.

Dry ice is carbon dioxide (CO_2) in its solid form. At temperatures above -56.4 °C, dry ice changes directly from a solid to a gas, without ever being a liquid. This process is called sublimation.

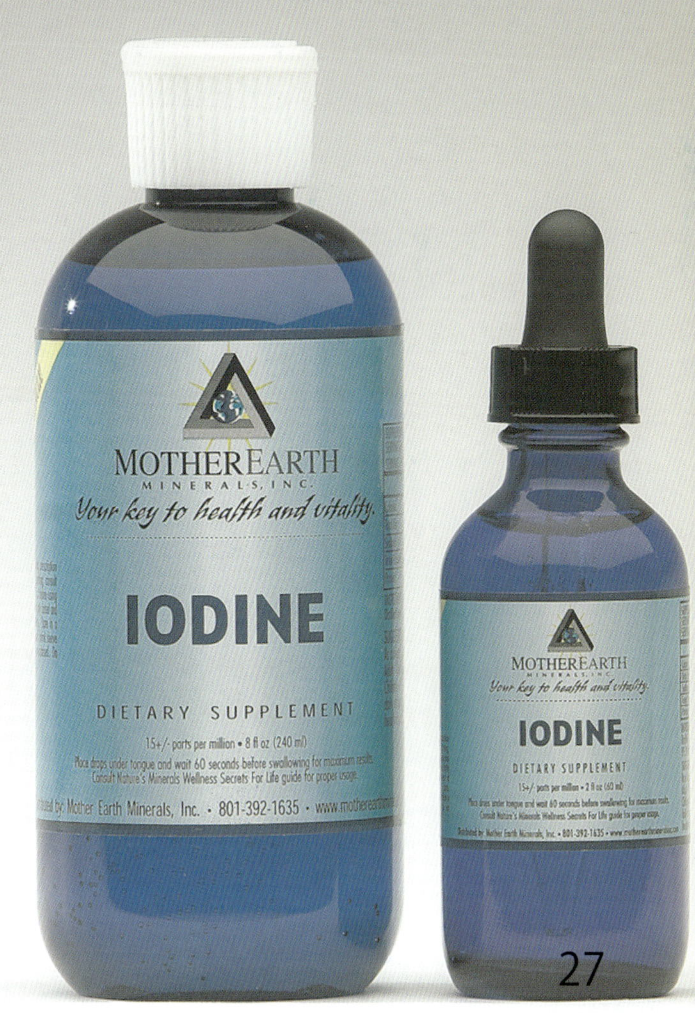

Platinum

78
Pt
195.08

Platinum is a transition metal. It has a concentration of approximately 10^{-6} per cent in the Earth's crust. The pure metal is malleable and ductile. It is lustrous and silvery in appearance. It is capable of absorbing gaseous hydrogen. Platinum is found in nature in alluvial deposits and in association with copper, iron and nickel sulphide ores. It was discovered by Antonio de Ulloa and Don Jorge Juan y Santacilia in 1735. Charles Wood independently isolated the element in 1741.

Platinum is used as a catalyst in a wide variety of chemical reactions. Some of the more common catalytic uses are the oxidation of organic vapours in automobile exhaust, the oxidation of ammonia in the production of nitric acid and the rearrangement of atoms in petroleum reforming. The common compounds formed by platinum are their halides. Most of the halides are formed by direct combination of the halogen elements with platinum. For example, PtF_6, $PtCl_4$, $PtBr_3$ and PtI_2. Platinum also forms two oxides, PtO and PtO_2, but they are unstable and decompose upon heating. Platinum forms coordination complexes (structures which consist of a central metallic atom, bonded to an array of surrounding molecules) with carbon, nitrogen, phosphorous, oxygen and sulphur donor atoms. The most well- known coordination complex of platinum is *cis* -platin, which is used in chemotherapy treatments of cancer.

Carbon monoxide (CO) is very toxic to both humans and animals. It forms in conditions when there is not enough oxygen to form carbon dioxide (CO_2). In many countries around the world, carbon monoxide poisoning is the most common kind of fatal poisoning.

Gold

79
Au
196.97

Gold is a soft yellow metal. The name of the element is derived from the Anglo-Saxon word geolo, meaning 'yellow'. It is the most malleable and ductile metal known. It is a good conductor of heat and electricity, and unreactive in air and most reagents. The relative abundance of gold is 0.004 parts per million in Earth's crust. Deposits of the metal are found in South Africa, Siberia, North America and South America. A modern method of isolation is the cyanide process, in which gold is leached from crushed rock with an aerated solution of sodium cyanide. The gold then precipitates upon addition of zinc dust and is purified by electrolytic refining.

Gold is commonly used for ornamental purposes such as jewellery and plating. It is a component of electrical connectors in computer equipment due to its high electrical conductivity. Its unreactivity in air leads to its use for corrosion-free contacts in electrical connections. As an excellent conductor of heat, it is used in the main engine nozzle of the space shuttle. Since gold is the most reflective of all metals, it is used as a coating for space satellites, face shields and windows. The most common compounds are gold chloride ($AuCl_3$) and chlorauric acid ($HAuCl_4$). Chlorauric acid is used in photography.

Mercury

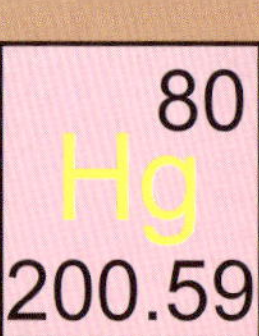

Mercury is a transition metal. It is silver in colour and unlike other metals, it is liquid at room temperature. Mercury's presence in the Earth's crust is relatively low compared to other elements. However, mercury is not considered rare because it is found in large, highly concentrated deposits. Mercury exists in the form of a red ore called cinnabar, which is composed of mercury and sulphur. It is relatively easy to extract from the ore by applying heat and a filtration process. First the ore is heated in an oxygen furnace. The ancient name for mercury was quicksilver. This name reflects mercury's lustrous silver colour and its unusually lively behaviour. When it is poured onto a smooth surface, it forms beads that roll rapidly around. No one knows exactly when mercury was discovered, but many ancient civilizations were familiar with this element. In Roman times, people had learned to extract mercury from its ore and used it to purify gold and silver. Ore containing gold or silver would be crushed and treated with mercury, which rejects impurities, to form a mercury alloy, called an amalgam. When the amalgam is heated, the mercury vaporizes, leaving pure gold or silver.

The most important use of mercury is in the preparation of chlorine. Chlorine is produced by passing an electric current through sodium chloride. It is used in switches and other electrical applications. It is also used in dental applications, measuring instruments (such as mercury thermometers and barometers), and coatings for mirrors. It forms many compounds with other elements which have wide applications. Mercuric cyanide (Hg (CN)2) is used in germicidal soaps and photography. Mercurous chloride (Hg2Cl2) is used as fungicide and in fireworks. Mercurous iodide (Hg2I2) kills bacteria on the skin.

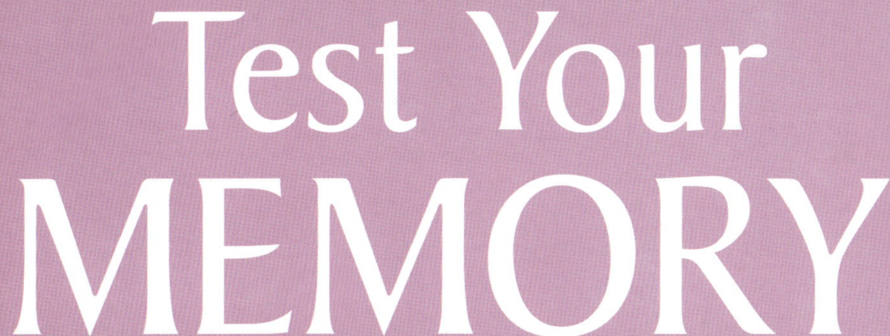

1. What is the difference between compounds and mixtures?
2. Give a brief account of the periodic table.
3. What are the periodic trends of elements?
4. What are the various element groups?
5. Define electro-negativity.
6. What do you know about hydrogen?
7. Give some chemical properties of carbon.
8. Name any three halogens.
9. What are noble gases?
10. Write some important uses of silver.
11. What are the transition elements?
12. What is the name of mercury ore?

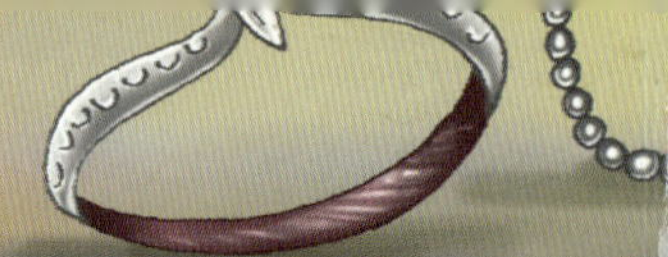

Index

A

actinides 14
alkali metals 10, 11, 12, 13
amalgam 26, 30
analytic reagent 26
antimony 12, 25, 26
atoms 4, 8, 9, 15, 16, 18, 28

B

Beryllium 21
bromine 11, 17, 23

C

catalyst 26, 28
catenation 18
chemotherapy 28

D

ductile 10, 22, 28, 29

E

electron 5, 6, 8, 9, 12, 13, 15

H

halogens 9, 11, 12, 17, 23, 24, 27
heterogeneous 4
homogeneous 4
hydrogenation 17

I

ionization 6, 9, 10, 11, 12, 13

L

lanthanides 14

M

malleability 3, 10
malleable 10, 28, 29
mercury 10, 17, 23, 26, 30

N

noble gases 3, 9, 11
nucleus 8, 9, 13, 24

O

oxidation 13, 20, 24, 28
oxidizers 20

R

radioactive isotope 18
rare Earths 13, 14

S

solutions 4, 13, 27
sublimation 27

T

transition metals 13, 25

V

valence electrons 6, 8, 9, 10, 11, 13